One Hundred Years of Fash

By Kelly Horton

For any further details, including information on other books or colouring pages contact:

Kellyartistthorton@yahoo.com

For more colouring pages:

www.etsy.com/uk/Colourcollectiveshop

For Video Tutorial search you tube:

The Colour Collective

~Dedication~

Firstly, a Thank you to my supportive Family, My husband and our five children, who are always encouraging, supportive, and are always there to help and advice creatively.

Secondly, a special Thank you to my Colouring team, whom have been colouring my pages, and providing feedback throughout the process of creating this book. I thank you for your hard work, your enthusiasm and your loyalty.

And finally Thank you to you, the colourist. Without your passion for colouring I could not create these books. The colouring community has welcomed me with open arms, and in return, I hope to create books that continue to give you enjoyment.

One Hundred Years Of fashion

Victorian Era 1837-1901

Edwardian Era 1901-10

King George 1910-1936

This colouring book focusses on the English fashion trends throughout the 100 years of the Victorian era, Edwardian era and the reign of King George.

The Edwardian Era is the last Era to be named after the Monarch that reigned during that period of time. Although King Edward VII reign ended in 1910, and King George was crowned, it is considered by most historians that the Edwardian era continued up to the outbreak of the First World war in 1914.

The Victorian and Edwardian Era has been well documented over the years through the use of plays, theatre, novels, films and TV. The lifestyle and Fashions of the Victorian and Edwardian era has always interested myself and captivated audiences all over the world.

The Victorian era brought great General, Economic, finance, social, education, technological, cultural and creative change. Fashion has played a large part in reflecting the changing attitudes and behaviours of the populous as the country moved through great change during Queen Victoria's reign, until the Reign of King George.

The country saw political reform, the abolishment of slavery, expanding industries, and railway lines, income tax, and a better health and education system. The country was shocked and devastated by the sinking of the Titanic, and the country fought through the Crimean, and Boer wars, and finally they fought in World War I.

This time period changed the way that Britain had lived in so many ways. The aristocrats found themselves with less power and influence, especially when the first labour party took power, and the changing political system to allow for more voters. It took a number of years but eventually the single woman over the age of 18 could vote, and this played a massive part in the fashions of the 1920's.

The changing world constantly affected fashion, fashion magazines were predominantly aimed at women, as they still are today, and these magazines and fashion designers were able to sense the changing attitudes and changing cultures of Britain over these years. They catered their ideas to the way in which the country was changing, an so fashion affected the population, as did the populous opinion and behaviours affect fashion. Throughout these one hundred years I have illustrated not just the fashions of the time, but also researched the historical, cultural, and society changes that affected the fashions. Take a journey through the 100 years of Fashion, and not only colour these illustrations but also learn about the fashion and the changing culture of England's rich history.

1820-1830

The Romantic Era

Technically these were the last few years of the Romantic era, but fashion changed slowly during these years depending on where you lived in England.

The clothing was very feminine and flowing. Although the ladies still wore corsets, the dresses were not fitted too tight to the bodice, as they would be in future years. The corset and dresses still gave a feminine V shape to the body, creating the first 19th century idea of the "hour glass" figure.

The neckline dropped and became wider, and the clothes were ornate in detail. The ankle length skirts became larger and fuller, using multiple petticoats to create the fuller look. The shoulders and arms of the dresses also became fuller, creating the "puff" sleeve.

The fashion trend of the larger dresses affected the outerwear for winter and colder weather. Because the dresses were fuller, it was impossible to wear a fitted coat, and so capes became popular. The capes would be made of heavier materials for the colder seasons and depending upon the ladies' finances, they could be lined with animal fir to keep the lady warmer.

Ladies always wore hats and gloves outside of the home, except for evening wear, the hats would change depending upon the season too.

Evening dresses were decorated to excess, the more ornately detailed, the more important and the more money you had. The English aristocracy did not discuss money, but they liked to show off that they had money, and status.

The women were wearing dresses that were off the shoulder to show the décolletage during the evening. Whether dining at home or dining out, the ladies still changed out of their day clothes and dressed to impress every night.

The jewellery was dropped ear rings, of pearl, gold, or diamonds. Worn with ornate, and delicate necklaces and rings. Gloves would be worn over the jewellery if it was anticipated that the lady would be taking them off during the evening. If the event required for the lady to keep her gloves on, then she would wear larger jewellery over the gloves.

The dresses were made with lace, silk, embroidery, pleats and gathers to excess, making them beautifully detailed and ornate. The colours of the dresses were dependent upon which style the dress was made for.

Day dresses were often pastel colours, with light embroidery, flowers, and feminine lace, whereas the evening dresses would be richer colours, deep reds, blue, golds, and purples, these would be decorated heavier, more embroidery, more gathers, trimmed in silk, and crystals so that the ladies' sparkled in candle light.

The ladies' hair was also ornately wrapped into a chignon, with a parting in the centre of the head, and ringlets draped either side of the face. Feathers, flowers and jewels were all worn in the hair.

Make up was worn during this time but was not worn as heavy as the French aristocracy. The use of Rouge during the French revolution was popular in England but was used in a natural way. Rouge would be used on the lips and cheeks, but the English aristocracy did not use the white powders that were so popular in France. The ladies' magazine's popular in this day emphasised the importance of natural beauty and gave advice to aristocracy on fashion, make up and etiquette. These magazines even went so far as to suggest that ladies who wore heavy make-up were not "innocent or wholesome" ladies.

The Romantic Era was all about natural, and feminine beauty.

The fashion of the 1830's continued into the 1840's with subtle changes as the decade moved forward. The fashion changed only slightly, with more emphasis being on the ladies' figures. Lower sloping shoulders and necklines were now popular.

The puff shoulders were all bigger in size. The dresses became tighter fitted to accentuate the ladies' figures. The corsets were longer, creating a low pointed waist. The skirts became even bigger, known as "bell skirts". These skirts were now structured with even more petticoats to create a much larger shape.

The overall shape of the dress was creating the hour glass figure, and a larger higher bosom was desired, with a very small waist. If you were not lucky enough to have this figure naturally, the undergarments, and corsets would help to achieve this shape.

Shawls and capes were still worn as outer layers to accommodate the size of the shoulders, the shawls were an important part of the outfit for the aristocracy. They were intricately crocheted for the warmer months, and made of heavier materials, ornately decorated for the winter months.

The hair was still very similar with only small changes. The hair was still parted in the middle, with ringlets down the side of the face, but it was now fashionable to plait the hair and arrange around the ears, before meeting at the back to be secured in a chignon.

Make up was again very similar, with emphasis on natural beauty. Ladies were encouraged to have good personal cleanliness and grooming, such as eyebrow shaping, and facial masks. Facial masks would be made of natural ingredients, such as fruit and flowers, all of which that would be appealing to the aristocracy.

1860-1870

The Gothic Era

Fashion changed considerably during the 1860's, fashion no longer represented the romantic, delicate, feminine era, the fashion became harsher and more restrictive.

The day dresses featured tight corsets and bodices with high necks and button fronts. Lace was used to frame the neck collars, or to line the blouse, but the fashion was no longer overly feminine. Day dresses had changed colours, these were darker, richer colours, usually not as ornately decorated as the evening fashions.

The neck line remained low during the evening fashions, but the shoulders had lost their volume and became fitted. The skirt hems lowered right to the floor covering the ladies buckled shoes, or boots. The skirts were worn higher on the waist, and were lower at the back of the skirts, dragging behind them.

The cage crinoline or the Hoop came onto the scene in the late 1850's and were now extremely popular, and used to change the shape of the ladies' silhouette and help create the shape of the skirts that were desired. The overall female shape was no longer the hour glass, but was an S -shape. The skirt shape was domed, and larger at the back, more petticoats than before were worn, with ornately decorated swags and layers to add additional volume. The new cage delighted women as it was able to support the weight of the numerous petticoats and the huge number of undergarments and layers of fabric to create such a silhouette.

The crinoline became a standard part of every ladies' wardrobe, from the upper-class ladies to the middle class, shop workers and maids. It was considered to be the only way to dress during this time period, it was an essential part of the ladies' wardrobe. Until the late 1870's where the shape of the crinoline and hoop changed to an oval shape. This became popular in the 1880's.

The hair was similar to previous years, parted in the centre again, with looser curls or ringlets down the sides of the face. The plaits and hair were wrapped ornately around the head and secured tightly at the nape of the neck in a low chignon. Ostrich feathers, pomegranate flowers, and silk butterflies were now popular to be worn in the hair, they signified the ladies' wealth and importance.

Outerwear had returned to dress coats, with smaller shoulders that could fit inside a coat, it was made with a split up the back of the coat and slightly elongated at the back to cover the larger skirts.

Toward the end of 1870 to 1880 the hairstyles were becoming bigger in volume and were placed on the head a little higher and without a prominent parting.

The make-up was now worn with a little more extravagance, the rouge was in different shades, and so the lips would be accentuated more, and the cheeks would have a natural glow.

Jewellery worn was also more extravagant, the diamonds and pearls were larger, and the designs more intricate. The ladies always wore day jewellery, which was smaller, and less extravagant but the evening jewellery was larger, more expensive and worn to excess. Earrings, necklaces, bracelets, and rings were all very popular.

1880-1890

The end of the 1870's brought the oval hoop to the skirts, changing the shape from the all-round voluminous skirts with a longer train of skirts at the back, to a flatter skirt at the front. The Bustle was used to place the emphasis on the back, creating the higher rounder, and fuller skirts. The bustle was a structural framework to support all of the materials, swags and undergarments at the back of the skirt to keep that desired shape. The Bustle will remain a popular and essential part of a ladies wardrobe for many years.

The dresses became even more complicated with a profusion of puffs, ruching, and trimmings. Ribbons, drapery and flounces were used at the back of the skirt, creating elaborate layers of materials. The back of the skirts became so long and so full that they were compared to a peacock's tail, trailing behind the lady as she walked.

The time period of the 1890's brought big change to ladies' fashions, the decline of the bustle and large hoops brought simpler flatter skirts, in an A-line style. The desired shape was now the hourglass again, instead of the S shape created in the previous years.

With decline of the bustle, the sleeves began to grow again, horizontal decoration on the bodice was used to elongate the body and teamed with higher waisted A-line skirts.

Toward the end of the 1890's masculine tailoring and simpler styles were becoming increasingly popular. For day wear, Women were beginning to wear clothes that were more functional, such as shirts and blouses with collars, and even sometimes with a tie.

Evening dresses were still as extravagant as ever, echoing fashion of earlier periods. The dresses were hour glass in shape, with large full skirts. Corsets were used to accentuate a small waist, while the neck lines were low and sweeping. As with all of the fashions the materials and patterns changed with the seasons, from light chiffons, and pastel colours, to dark heavier velvets and richer colours. The sleeves ranged from large puffy shoulders, to slimmer more fitted sleeves. This time period gave more choice to the ladies with many elements from previous years being brought back into fashion.

The hairstyles were now higher in volume, wavy, and worn higher on the head, and pinned into a loose chignon. Curls were left to fall around the face, and usually the hair did not have a parting, as the hair was worn high.

During the evening, as in previous years, the hair was ordained with small accessories such as flowers, beads, and feathers.

1900-1910

The S bend corset was now very fashionable, it pushed the hips backward, but forced the chest forward, bringing emphasis to the bosom. This was emphasised further with frilly details on blouses that were embellished with lace and ribbons. The elongated skirts at the back were still fashionable but without the full padding and voluminous layers. The overall fashion trend had lost its volume, the skirts and sleeves were now streamlined and flatter.

The day wear was usually separates, shirts or blouses teamed with A-line skirts at ankle length. With evening wear continuing to be dresses.

The fashion was changing and becoming more practical, women were participating in more activities that need more practical clothing. And although the clothes were more practical even for the aristocratic ladies they still had beautiful embellishments and details that made them stand out from the lower classes.

The undergarments were worn mostly for modesty, and not for structural use.

Hair was once again similar to the previous years, tied lower in a chignon during the day, with soft waves and loose curls, to a higher, more ornately decorated chignon, with ringlets and decoration for evening wear.

The country was slowly changing to move with the countries growing needs, but the change that was about to happen in the next few years could never have been predicted.

The whole population would be affected by the First World War, but not how the government quite expected them to be.

And with all change, fashion was a massive influencer to the way in which women decided they wanted to live.

The First World War began on 28th July 1914 and ended four years later on 11th November 1918.

The affects of this war rippled through every household, from the very poor to the very rich. No one was safe, every young man was sent to war and many, many did not return.

The absence of working men in the country meant that households needed to find another way to support themselves. Women had to go to work, they needed to provide for their family, and so they stepped up, and became the earner of the family, as well as their other duties.

Because of the extra duties that all women had taken on, they needed more practical clothing, they could not wear overtly large, frilly, and impractical clothes. And so, the Fashion of the 1910 finally ended the large, extravagant ball gowns, and we can see in the clothes of 1910 some similarities of what we may wear today.

Not only did fashion change during the years before and after WWI, but women changed, they had realised that they didn't need men, they were not the "weaker sex", they were in fact strong. They were intelligent, they were hard working, and they deserved to have a voice. They deserved to be listened to, not only in their own homes, but also outside, in the world. Women wanted the right to vote. And they were determined to get it.

The fashions from 1910-1930 represented, in my opinion, the original "girl power" movement ,women were going to be listened to, and they would demand it!

1920-1930

The roaring twenties and the Flapper era

The end of the First World war brought great change. Not only did the country lose so many young men, but they gained many strong women. The "lower classes" had decided that they had fought for their country and now they demanded more for their sacrifice.

The aristocracy was losing power and influence, no longer did the public look up to them. The average working man could now work, earn money and become a self-made man, it didn't matter that he was not from a high-class family. This attitude spread throughout the country, even more so when a labour party took Government control.

There were many jobs to be had, and women were now working, and moving up in the business world.

A working man, Husband and Father could now own his own business, buy his own home, and this new-found freedom affected his wives and daughters. He gained power and so did they. No longer was the working man forever classed as a lower classed citizen, he could make a real change to his and his families lives. They demanded better, better education, better healthcare, better opportunities, and more respect.

Women were finally making decisions for themselves, they were taking charge of their families and their businesses. They were choosing whom they marry, and choosing how they live and as time moved on, their fashion would reflect their rebellious attitude.

The women of the 1920's were hard working independent women, this is where the flapper era began.

The women were celebrating their new roles, and demonstrating their independence and power with looser fitted, drop waisted and shorter dresses. After WWI it is believed that the country entered a euphoria of celebrating life, and so behaviours were sometimes shocking to older generations of the time. Younger people were drinking, smoking, dancing, listening to jazz, and expressing more opinions than ever before.

The ladies wore shorter dresses, showing their ankles and legs, and as the years go on, they wore dresses above the knee. Which was shocking considering the fashions only a few years earlier.

Glamour and sparkle was most popular for evening wear. The ladies wore loose undergarments with no structure, with loose silk dresses, adorned with embroidery, jewels or tassels. They also wore head dresses with feathers and flowers.

The dresses were revealing in comparison to previous years, the shoulders were small straps, and low cut, showing far more skin than ever before.

The ladies were now wearing stockings that could be seen. because of the high dress lines and were worn with sparkling shoes with buckles and laces and high heels.

The hair and make-up also changed.

No longer did women feel they must have the "natural look" they were longing to look like the stars from the theatres, photo plays and musicals. They were wearing darker lipsticks, mascaras, eye shadows, and face powders.

The ladies also radically changed their hair. They cut their hair into a bob style, finger waved and gelled their hair. If they were not brave enough to cut their hair, it was styled in finger waves and tied at the nape of neck.

Everything about the fashions of the 1920's and 1930's was about the countries youth celebrating life, celebrating freedom and celebrating the opportunity for change. This was especially true for women. Women demonstrated their new-found confidence through fashion and united the countries female population to fight for the right to vote. Although it came in stages, by 1928, right in the height of the flapper era, women won the right to vote as equals to their male counterparts. The 1920's will always be regarded by myself and many others as the first real "Girl Power" movement.

THE DANCE

Bonnet's and shoes

Made in the USA
Lexington, KY
13 June 2019